For Your Garden

WINDOW BOXES

For Your Garden

WINDOW BOXES

Carol Spier

Little, Brown and Company
Boston New York Toronto London

First Edition

Library of Congress Cataloging-in-Publication Data
Spier, Carol.
        Window boxes/Carol Spier.—1st ed.
            p. cm.—(For your garden)
        "A Friedman Group book"—T.p. verso.
        ISBN 0-316-80824-5
        1. Window gardening. 2. Window gardening—Pictorial works.
        I. Title. II. Series.
        SB419. S594 1994
        717—dc20   93-22413

A FRIEDMAN GROUP BOOK
10 9 8 7 6 5 4 3 2 1
Published simultaneously in Canada by Little, Brown & Company (Canada) Limited

FOR YOUR GARDEN: WINDOW BOXES
was prepared and produced by
Michael Friedman Publishing Group, Inc.
15 West 26th Street
New York, New York 10010

Editor: Kelly Matthews
Art Directors: Jeff Batzli and Lynne Yeamans
Designer: Stan Stanski
Photography Director: Christopher C. Bain

Printed and bound in Hong Kong by Leefung-Asco Printers Ltd.

Table of Contents

INTRODUCTION

*W*indow boxes are like grace notes, accenting a composition of landscape and architecture with charm, whimsy, dignity, or color. Small gardens set above the ground, window boxes trim and finish a facade the way a bouquet or a dried flower arrangement finishes a room's decor, enhancing its style and creating or emphasizing a mood by their shape, color, and demeanor. In addition, they bring a bit of prettily tilled soil within reach of inhabitants, complete with bees, butterflies, occasional birds, and the thrills and vagaries of seasonal gardening that simply are not offered by house plants.

In cities or in towns where the homes are built right up against the sidewalks, window boxes may offer residents their only opportunity to have a garden, and they also serve to soften the appearance of the landscape. In more rural settings, window boxes provide a link between lawn and home, complementing and extending the gardens below. Boxes can be sophisticated or rustic in design, permanently or seasonally displayed, formally or informally planted. You can grow flowers, small shrubs, vines, and herbs in window boxes, depending upon the seasonal effects desired, location of the box, and climate in which you live. In addition, your plantings may be annual or perennial.

Window boxes from many different settings have been gathered here. Some are straightforward, others are fanciful, adorning a home such as yours or such as you might dream of. You may choose to interpret some boxes for your own landscape, while others may not be appropriate, but all should please on the merit of their existing charm.

INTEGRATING WINDOW BOXES WITH YOUR LANDSCAPE

When you add a window box to your home, it should be in keeping with the style of the facade and landscape. Window boxes are usually charming, but there is a fine line between charming and trite, and not every dwelling will be enhanced by elevated boxes of blooms. As you consider whether to add window boxes and what

type of box and plantings to use, look around your neighborhood and in architecture, gardening, and travel books and magazines for ideas that please you, and note as well any boxes that seem inappropriate in their settings. You want your box to enhance your home, not to gussy it up, so balance the style and size of the box and the shape and color of the plantings with the style, color, and proportions of your home and landscape.

ABOVE: This Federal-style home sits just a step away from the sidewalk, and the tiny yard permits just a bit of foundation planting. The small green window boxes continue the orderly trim of the shutters. Filled with trailing ivy and lantana, they give a soft finish to this very proper dwelling.

OPPOSITE: There is no room for front-yard gardens on this block of town houses, but each sill holds a window box that softens the formal expanse of brick. The quiet, monochromatic plantings are in keeping with the elegant architecture but bring a humanizing hint of domesticity to the urban setting. Even a small touch of gardening seems to give a neighborhood a residential character; window boxes placed on city shops, as well as homes, will appear welcoming to passersby.

LEFT: In older European cities, it is quite common to find stone houses built one against the other along narrow streets. Rarely blessed with front gardens, they can present a cold and rather gloomy face when left unadorned—which is not very often. One sees lovingly tended window boxes bringing color and life to nearly every sill for as much of the year as weather permits.

BELOW: In a suburban setting, window boxes are likely to be combined with other landscape details. This Tudor-style home sits comfortably among mature trees and shrubs and in spring is surrounded by lavish blooms. The window boxes soften the dark facade and sharply contrasting white trim and carry the spring flowers charmingly but discreetly up to every floor.

ABOVE: Dozens of red geraniums provide the only note of color found on the facade of this large and handsome Colonial Revival house, with dozens more lining the walkway. Such an unbroken expanse of white adds a touch of severity to the formality of the architecture; the regularly repeating red offers a bit of wanted but appropriately controlled relief.

ABOVE: The sun beats unrelentingly on the stone houses at the top of this ancient hillside village in rural France. Although the houses are closely spaced and it is too steep to garden here easily, the residents managed to establish a small plot of flowers and train a great grapevine over the streetside doorway. The fanciful ironwork is bravely lighthearted against the heavy stone; the lovely curved balconet, never intended for human occupation, makes a luxurious window box.

RIGHT: The front of this small country home is shaded by a porch that keeps direct light from the windows, so a window box fills the bay over the porch rail instead. The walkway up to the steps is dotted with small planters; the vines trailing from the box carry the eye from one charming mound of blooms to the next.

OPPOSITE: This Tudor-style village home rises above a narrow, cobbled courtyard that offers little space for gardening. This is a sunny spot, however, and the hard aspect of stone and stucco is cheered by the sprightly dahlias, exuberantly climbing roses, and boxes of cascading geraniums.

ABOVE: In an open rural setting where the first view of a building may be from afar, the window plantings must be bold enough to hold their own against the architecture. The window bays of the porch along the front of this old Alpine granary are filled with boxes of red ivy geraniums, each spilling a strong band of color over the railings.

LEFT: This rustic shed has grown into its setting over time, weathering to the wonderful muted gray that is the perfect backdrop for pink and purple blossoms waving amid soft greenery. The box that sits unpretentiously below the primitive windows echoes their strong horizontal line with another in pink and green.

ABOVE: If your windows are long and close to the ground, then your window box plantings can relate directly to whatever is growing below. The brick terrace backing this home is lined with the variously colored and textured greenery of potted herbs; the rosemary in the box in the window reaches down to them. Imagine the fragrance when this window is raised.

RIGHT: Although we tend to think of window boxes as ornaments for the front of a house, they can just as happily trim the back, and if the back gardens are extensive, boxes can carry the plantings gaily up the wall. Here, a marvelous terrace is framed on three sides by a showy English border, and the back of the house acts as the fourth with the window boxes and hanging baskets integrating the wall with its landscape.

ABOVE: Great masses of real blooms dance before trompe l'oeil woodwork and frescoed scenes from a passion play in this special setting. Even though you might shy away from the pictorials, the painted trim is not inappropriate—or unattainable—for a stucco building, and the window boxes simply enhance the illusion.

OPPOSITE: Admittedly, a house edged by water may not be the norm, but if this happens to be your situation, take advantage of the water's reflective surface; any detail that is charming once is doubly so when mirrored. Here, lush geraniums tumble out of three windows twice.

Chapter One

WHAT KIND OF BOX?

The look of the box you place in your window may be as important to you as the plantings that will fill it, or if your plan calls for it to be obscured by the vegetation, your only concerns may be price, weight, and durability. When you shop for window boxes, you will see that they are available to suit every fanciful whim and fit any sophisticated style of architecture— for a price. There are, however, many good-looking and possibly more durable models to be found in most hardware or gardening supply stores. If you are handy with a hammer and saw, you can easily build your own.

Keep in mind that window boxes must have good drainage to prevent rot and that they will be heavy when filled, so be sure to consider how you will secure them to your house. Although terra-cotta and wood are very attractive, they do not always survive extremes of damp or temperature, so if you plan to leave your boxes out year-round, be sure they are fabricated and finished appropriately for your climate. You may find that a box made of metal, fiberglass, or a polymer will be a better investment, and if interestingly painted or when viewed from the street, you may not be able to tell the difference.

ABOVE: If copper is left to weather naturally, it takes on a wonderful verdigris patina that is complementary to most foliage and flowers. This look of natural antiquity is presently in vogue, and if you can't manage a real copper box, you might buy a do-it-yourself verdigris faux-finishing kit that will simulate the look on a number of other materials.

OPPOSITE: It is difficult to say whether it is the pressed-metal window boxes or drainpipe that is most charming here; certainly one complements the other—and the masonry—beautifully. The boxes are supported by sturdy but elegant brackets.

ABOVE: Paint can really dress up a wood box and help it to weather the elements. The color of course is a matter of personal preference; here, brilliant red makes a bold accent out of a humble box, setting off fuchsia and white blooms with aplomb.

OPPOSITE: Unfinished wood lends rustic charm to a window box. Here, five weathered boards were crudely banged together; this box makes no pretense to elegance but is very charming in this setting.

OPPOSITE: On this traditional clapboard home neat bands of contrasting molding finish a tailored window box with just enough sophistication to suit its surprisingly ornate supporting bracket. The cool and unified paint scheme keeps the effect low-key as foliage, living and ornamental, casts graceful shadows.

ABOVE: Spanning the length of a large picture window, this classic square-edged wooden box is so long that it needs to rest on sturdy brackets. There is nothing fancy about a homemade box such as this, but once painted to match the window trim and filled with robust plants, it is unobtrusive, serviceable, and good-looking.

OPPOSITE: A hollowed log makes a witty and perfectly appropriate window box to attach to a log house. The more this one weathers, the more it will have the aspect of an overgrown fallen branch in a woodland glade.

ABOVE: Flat-backed baskets make charming hanging planters—or window boxes. They bring an exuberant, informal sparkle to this rustic building. Baskets are easy to find, hang, and plant, but as they age, check the bottoms to make sure they are not rotting out.

ABOVE: Absorbent terra-cotta is of course an ideal material for flowerpots or any other sort of planter. Not all terra-cotta can withstand freezing, but otherwise, it is durable and weathers well. Terra-cotta is available in myriad styles—from the simple troughs sitting on this stone sill to more intricate and fancifully cast pieces—and its warm, rusty tones evoke visions of the Mediterranean wherever it is found.

OPPOSITE: Cast stone is a traditional material for all sorts of garden ornament; it weathers well and complements most foliage. It is durable and fairly inexpensive, but heavy. Boxes of cast stone may be very simple or quite elegant. This lovely footed box brings a wonderful element of profusion to its overgrown setting.

ABOVE: In some forms of architecture, brackets, often made of ornamental ironwork, extend above the sill to form a window guard called a balconet. A balconet can be fanciful or elaborate, like the semi-circular one on page 11, or simple. The one surrounding this box is just a simple fence of uprights that breaks up the long plain surface of the terra-cotta. This locale is so overgrown with ivy that anything more elaborate would be lost.

LEFT: Window boxes are sometimes partially obscured by brackets that form a cage around them. When this is the case, the brackets are usually more interesting to look at than the boxes, which should be plain so as not to interfere. This simple green box sits on a shelf that is fenced with miniature pickets; the ivy geraniums tumbling over them look like rambling roses along a full-size garden fence.

ABOVE: If your windows are especially pretty or interestingly trimmed, an ornate window box might detract from their inherent charms. To keep the focus on the architecture, choose a plain box and let the plantings obscure it with a soft, colorful accent—as does the froth of ivy geraniums at this scroll-embellished corner.

ABOVE: A row of pots lining a sill gives an effect similar to that of a true window box, and has the advantage of easy transfer indoors when the season turns. Oddly assorted pots lend a casual ambiance, so choose matching ones if a formal display is preferred—and be sure your sill is deep and level enough to house them securely.

Chapter Two

A MATTER OF STYLE

s with any other form of gardening, the design of a window garden may be formal or informal, and there are a number of factors that determine which look is appropriate to a particular location. Often, the architectural style of the building will set the tone, indicating the style of both box and plantings, but just as often, the whim of the gardener can steer the choice, creating a soft and naturalistic box for a row house or one that observes some formal rule of color or shape for a cottage. As you decide, consider how the different looks would complement your home and what sort of mood they would convey. If you feel unsure of your design talents, it is never wrong to stick with the traditional, but remember that window boxes are small, and unless you are installing a lot of them, you can experiment with different looks without making a huge investment of time or money. In addition, there are times when the distinction between formal and informal becomes purely subjective, so concentrate on creating a box that pleases you, trust your instincts, remember that a formal garden design is only as good as maintenance keeps it, and have fun.

FORMAL PLANTINGS AND BOXES

Formal window boxes are most often seen on formal buildings in urban locations. The boxes can be plain or embellished with architectural details—perhaps repeating a motif seen elsewhere on the building—and they can be made of almost any material with a plain or natural finish or perhaps a fancy painted one. While they ought not to be not folkloric or rustic, they might have an antique patina or a shadow of moss.

Formal plantings follow a regular, orderly plan, usually one that relies upon symmetry of shape and color to provide balance. It is not so much the type of plants chosen as the way they are arranged that gives a box a formal demeanor, although you are more likely to use small shrubs or topiaries in a formal rather than an informal box, and some climbing and cascading plants have an exuberance that sets an informal tone.

ABOVE: The rim of this stone balconet is lined with plain boxes, each of which holds two cyclamens with elegant blooms erect above mounding foliage. The simple, regularly punctuated bands made by boxes, leaves, and flowers provide just the right accent for the complex facade behind them; the lobed blossoms pay a nice compliment to the trefoil arches topping the windows.

OPPOSITE: A carved and painted peacock, a formal bird if ever there was one, stands in proud display on this otherwise simple box. Three regularly spaced mounds of ivy have been trained over wire forms. The box is very subtle in this ivy-covered setting, with an aura of the antique and mysterious that is often found in old, shadowy formal gardens.

ABOVE: Although summery massed plantings soften the front of this London town house, they are arranged in an orderly manner; in the basket and each box, lobelia cascades below a mound of geraniums and petunias—blue below red and pink.

RIGHT: A massive building such as this stone retreat calls for a substantial rather than delicate window garden. Here, a great band of coleus rounds out the sill below the middle window bay and the vinca trails elegantly down to meet the ground cover. Coleus, which derives its quiet beauty from variegated leaves rather than showy blooms, is an apt choice to set in this dappled light against the strong texture of the stonework.

OPPOSITE: A plain white box continues the clean graphic effect of the pedimented window trim on this stuccoed building. Alyssum spills demurely over the front of the box; bright red geraniums appear dignified against their deep and variegated leaves in this pristine, controlled setting.

INFORMAL PLANTINGS AND BOXES

Informal window boxes lack the self-conscious control of formal ones—which doesn't mean that thought isn't given to their composition. They often contain a disparate assortment of plants that mingle with seeming abandon as they trail, climb, or spring from the box, but to be successful, the colors and shapes must be assembled with an eye toward harmony.

Informal window gardens can be planted in plain boxes or in rustic or earthy ones. An informal window garden may share the exuberance of a cottage garden, overflowing its plot so the box hardly shows, or its design may take its cue from the demeanor and material of the container, but it is unlikely that you would choose an elegantly ornamented box for a naturalistic planting.

OPPOSITE: Although most urban row houses have facades that are somewhat formal, they do not dictate the creation of formal window boxes unless they are built in a particularly mannered style. In fact, informal window gardens can soften the aspect of a town house. Here, unmatched gardens send sprightly horizontal bands of color splashing across a brick facade; though unalike, they are united by their shared overall shape and use of white and warm-colored blooms and trailing greens.

ABOVE: You need not mix a lot of plants or colors to create an informal window garden. Bright blue trim gives this small double window an unusual importance that is complemented by small, intensely yellow marigold blossoms peeking casually through a mass of feathery, dark green ferns.

ABOVE: In this wildly happy spot, it seems that a bit of everything that loves the sun has been gathered into one box. This garden works because the colors are well balanced and none of the plants has blooms or leaves that are overly large.

RIGHT: Snapdragons might seem an unusual choice to fill a window box, but they appear to be wonderfully happy here, giving this box the feeling of a full-blown country border. Taller stalks stand at lively attention to the sun above a mass of shorter snaps and violas; this mingling of intense colors is particularly pleasing.

OPPOSITE: Although the palette chosen for this rather sweet and maidenly planting is limited to pink, purple, and green and the arrangement is fairly orderly, the ivy trailing in and out of the dancing and cascading flowers breaks up the composition and gives it an informal air.

ABOVE: This window box has been filled with an informal gathering consisting mainly of herbs. The collection makes a wonderfully textured and fragrant mound of variegated green, and the effect is delicate and private rather than showy.

ABOVE: Here, lavish use of overflowing window boxes set amid rivulets of climbing ivy softens an otherwise severe facade. The composition of color and plants is repetitive, but the mood is carefree, not controlled.

OPPOSITE: If your home is sufficiently rustic or archaic in mood to support an abundance of exuberant window plantings, then let your green thumb run riot. Here, terra-cotta boxes and pots frame windows and doors, spilling jewel-toned blossoms in cheerful abandon over the old stones.

Chapter Three

A MATTER OF COLOR

Color may be the single most important design element in your window box. From a distance, you will notice the color of a composition before you are able to perceive anything else about it, and you will know at once if it is bright or pastel, cheery or demure, and probably whether it is a mass of a single color or a mix of many. You will also be able to tell immediately if the colors used in a window box flatter or clash with the facade they trim.

Color can suggest mood and attitude. The way colors are arranged can emphasize or create movement within a window box design. As you select your plants, think not only of their color and whether the blooms punctuate or obscure the foliage, but also of their growth habits—upright, mounding, cascading, or trailing—and of how you can work these elements together. Consider the length of a plant's blooming season, and whether you want to redo your box as the seasons change, or whether you would prefer something that will last from late spring to early autumn. Decide also if you would like a monochromatic box or one that is multicolored; either can be formal or informal, subtle or strong, and both are lovely.

MONOCHROMATIC PLANTINGS

Whether they are formal or informal in shape, subtle or dynamic in color, monochromatic window box plantings will generally provide an uncomplicated accent of color to a facade. By using only one color or one color plus foliage, you automatically simplify the number of elements that a viewer must absorb and your box will have a more graphic impact when seen from a distance. Up close you will be able to appreciate all the subtle variations of texture that might be lost in a melange of color.

ABOVE: The ivy geraniums twining through this wrought-iron window guard share its red color, and together they make a unified and delicate contrast to the white wall and lace curtain.

OPPOSITE: Red window trim brightens and punctuates the facade of this log home. By matching the geraniums to the paint, the impact of the box merges with that of the window as a single strong and graphic element.

ABOVE: Although not truly monochromatic, these boxes produce the initial impression of a great cascade of greenery softening the facade of the clapboard home they adorn. The foliage is far more important to this design than the flowers, and because the blooms match the shutters, they do not intrude upon the overall effect.

LEFT: Three ivy geraniums spill pink blossoms out of this large window. Because the geraniums are of the same type, the slight variation in their color does not distract from the impression of a pink cascade; it just adds a bit of life to the large display.

ABOVE: A boxful of herbs will always provide a study in subtle variations. Without the distraction of showy blossoms, one can take in all the curls, cuts, and velvets of the leaves, and the mounds, umbrellas, and cascades of the growth habits. A box as discreet as this would not have much impact when seen from halfway down the block, but it would add a graceful accent to a terrace or be a welcome addition on a kitchen sill.

ABOVE: A mass of wonderful egg-yolk yellow cheers this white box and window, picking up the warmth of the sunny brick wall around it. The choice of foliage is most appropriate, the yellow edge of the ivy complementing the rich blooms. (Scotch broom and chrysanthemums do not share a natural blooming season, so a box that duplicates this exactly must be intended for short-term display.)

ABOVE: A simple drape of deep blue lobelia is the perfect foil to the wonderful turquoise that colors real and trompe l'oeil trim on this California home. This window is so complex that it has no need for an elaborately designed planting; the choice made here is inspired.

OPPOSITE: Here, a lovely arrangement in white relies upon the differing sizes and textures of blooms for articulation. The white all but obscures the foliage, and the white-edged vinca continues the theme as it trails down the facade.

MULTICOLORED PLANTINGS

When you arrange a planting of colorful flowers, you have one of the most lavish paint boxes imaginable to work from. With the myriad hues and values available, you can create a window box that is impressionistic, graphic, vibrant, or controlled. You can select a palette that is warm or cool, made of complementary colors (from opposite sides of the color wheel) or analogous ones (neighbors on the color wheel). You can arrange a composition in which the colors follow some clearly marked pattern or mix them all together in a random manner.

The growing habits of the plants you choose will affect the way your arrangement matures, so think not only of the colors of the blossoms but of whether they appear on upright or trailing stems, whether they obscure their foliage or punctuate it, and whether a single specimen or a mass is needed to be most effective in your design. And don't neglect foliage plants; the greens available may be pure or tinted with yellow, gray, blue, and even red tones that complement or contrast different flowers in different ways.

ABOVE LEFT: The colors in this intimate window box were chosen for the rich value of their deep tones—egg-yolk yellow, purple, dark blue and green, and a bit of red—and arranged in small masses. Note how diminutive white and yellow blooms punctuate the composition.

ABOVE RIGHT: This half-round basket holds a sweet display of spring blooms—pansies, violas, impatiens, lobelia. All are delicately formed and richly hued, with just enough of each to make a pretty bouquet.

OPPOSITE: The window box taken, perhaps, to an extreme—but how magnificent. Here, tiers of hanging flower pots supplement the basic box and overflow with a melange of color and texture. This composition is not as haphazard as it first appears—it was planted symmetrically and arranged with an eye to texture and growth habit as well as color. As it matured, a marvelous mingling occurred.

ABOVE: Jewel-tone nasturtiums compose their own carefree display. Plant seeds from an assorted pack and you are guaranteed a balanced arrangement, complex and harmonious—and charming enough be the sole choice for a small box. Different types of nasturtiums trail, climb, or mound and have green or variegated foliage, so choose one that will grow as you desire.

OPPOSITE: Pink, purply blue, and white are the only colors set against the green in this small box. Blossoms of a different size and character were chosen for each color; the effect is simple and unpretentious but controlled.

OPPOSITE: A limited palette has been planted in controlled tiers of alternating color in this box, allowing the eye to appreciate each variation in texture and shape. These colors would be just as harmonious if arranged in a looser manner, but the mood of the composition would be quite different.

ABOVE: Daisies and lobelia are profuse bloomers with feathery foliage and gently disordered growth habits; here, they mingle charmingly in an impressionistic froth that softens the more intense pink of the geraniums that share the box.

Chapter Four

A MATTER OF LOCATION

*L*ight and climate, two influential conditions that are beyond the control of the gardener, affect the contents of window boxes as much as they do larger in-ground gardens. There are plants that thrive in shady conditions, others that require long hours of sun, and some that will thrive in either as long as they are properly watered. In the right climate, cacti, succulents, orchids, or bromeliads can be as wonderful in a window box as the more usual geraniums or impatiens. And no matter what the growing conditions, bright colors will make a location seem warmer, pale ones cooler. If you are in doubt as to what will be best for your location, consult a local nursery.

LEFT: This shady window is itself shaded by a curtain of pink, purple, and green. The window box is blanketed with impatiens but also holds climbing blooms, which twine toward the hanging basket of elegant fuchsia. Note how the medium-pink tones glow against the green in the dappled light.

OPPOSITE: Although impatiens are most often seen in shade or filtered light, they will survive in fairly sunny conditions as long as they don't get too hot and dry. Here, they mound prettily over a rustic box on a weathered board-and-batten wall.

ABOVE: As impatiens are a standard choice for shady windowsills, geraniums are ubiquitous on sunny ones. Luckily, they come in many shades of red, orange, and pink—and white as well—with upright or trailing growth habits and smooth, lobed, bright, and variegated leaves, so they offer lots of cheery possibility. Here, ivy geraniums spill out of casement windows onto an ivy-covered wall—a typical sight all over France.

LEFT: Begonias thrive in full sun or partial shade; here, their warm tones brighten a cool window.

ABOVE: A window in a wall bleached out by constant sun needs a box filled with strong colors that can stand up to the hot light. Lipstick, fuchsia, and egg yolk–colored flowers accent rich green foliage and hold their own on this bright sill.

OPPOSITE: Petunias are a classic choice for sunny window boxes. They come in white and almost any imaginable shade of red or blue; some varieties have striped petals that lend them a carnival air. Here, a soft melange of pink, lavender, and white blooms tumbles over an elegantly detailed box; the soft colors against the gray wood have a cooling effect on the sunny facade.

Chapter Five

A MATTER OF SEASON

*Y*ou may or may not wish to acknowledge the changing seasons in your window box designs—many gardeners prefer to wait till the spring sun warms enough to presage summer and then create a box that will last until frost. Of course, you may be one of those who simply cannot resist the first primroses and pansies and is prepared to trade them for something more heat-tolerant later in the season. And when frost knocks out your summer blooms, you may find a barren box unbearable and fill it with dwarf evergreens or a dried arrangement.

The climate in which you live and the overall nature of your landscaping will no doubt influence your choice of seasonal schemes. Some colors are naturally associated with certain seasons—pastels for spring, brights for summer, rich rusty tones for autumn, and evergreens for winter—but these associations are hardly rules. Springtime's yellows are as intense as any you might find in summer's flower beds, and there are as many pale pinks to be found in summer's sun and shade as there are in spring's first buds; so think first of the type of plants you wish to use, and then select colors that suit your mood.

ABOVE: Pansies and violas are full of simple springtime cheer—their determined little faces always indicate that warmer weather is on the way. This is a lovely use of tonal color in a mellow setting.

OPPOSITE: Fragrant, starry-eyed primroses make an appearance in hothouses soon after the winter solstice and are among the first flowers offered by nurseries in the spring. They are hardy outdoors year-round where winters are mild and will sometimes surprise you with blooms peeking up from leaf mulch and light snow. Planted with amaryllis in these beautiful cast-stone troughs, they offer a bright encouragement to springtime.

ABOVE: Even a quick glance at this joyful mound of hot colors lets you know—or feel—that high summer is at hand. Note that this lively arrangement has lots of red—and not a geranium in sight.

OPPOSITE: The flowers chosen for this small box will bloom from late spring until frost. This is a charming composition of contrasts—and contains a numerous variety for such a tiny spot.

ABOVE: Here is a very pretty, and slightly unexpected, arrangement of summer's classic blooms. The pendant fuchsia carry the hot red of the geraniums gaily down into the cooler purple of the lobelia, while the pale pink geraniums complement the stone panel below the box and pick up the light tone that accents the red and purple cascade.

ABOVE: As the days cool toward autumn, our eyes yearn for some of the same warmth our bodies find in sweaters and scarves. Chrysanthemums offer a soft and velvety blanket of russet tones; here, a band of small plants in full bloom nestles cozily against a windowsill.

OPPOSITE: A building with an impressive facade can carry a grand display of autumn color. Here, a magnificent blanket of gold and white chrysanthemums takes in the air on a balcony railing fronting stately French doors; like us, they seem to enjoy basking in the last warm light of the year.

ABOVE: Although the season for outdoor flowers passes with the coming of winter, there is no reason to let your window boxes stand naked and forlorn against the cold weather. Try planting small evergreens—perhaps topiary trained—in your boxes, or fill them with seasonal arrangements of dried naturals, cut greens, or a combination, as shown here. Remember that cut or dried arrangements need as much care—or more—as living ones, so don't abandon them to wind and snow, and don't let holiday displays outstay their purpose.